29

With best

from

[signature]

Keylines

Keylines

Ann Henning Jocelyn

DOONREAGHAN PRESS

Published in 2000
by Doonreaghan Press
Cashel, Co. Galway,
Ireland.

ISBN 0-9539033-0-3

Cover design by Doonreaghan Press
Printed in Dublin by Colour Books
Baldoyle, Dublin, Ireland.

CONTENTS

Birth

Have you heard about the birth myth?
It is supposed to hold the key
not so much to who you are,
as to who you think you are.

The birth myth is the story you've been told
about circumstances surrounding your birth.

It stands to reason that it makes a difference
if you were born after three days of protracted labour,
so agonising that your mother vowed
never to bear another child,
and never did.

Or if you were the long-awaited heir
hailed as a gift from heaven,
whose birth was celebrated
in floods of champagne?

Or the unwanted fruit
of a shameful illicit liaison,
born after a failed termination
to your mother's bitter grief.

Or perhaps you were the seventh out of ten,
who slipped into the world almost unnoticed?
So insignificant, even your family
can't recall much about it.

Or a weakling saved against the odds
amidst much tears and anguish:
a triumph of life over affliction?

Often it is nothing but a myth;
sometimes quite unfounded.
But it still reveals a lot
about your own perceptions.

Now you know what the birth myth is.
The question is – what is yours?

August, 1948.
A hospital in Gothenburg, Sweden.
A young doctor, himself a patient,
in a bare room,
nearing the end of a losing battle
against leukaemia.

Next to him, his wife:
younger still, looking like a school-girl,
except for the fact
that she is nine months pregnant.

They are waiting,
as they have waited these last seven months,
for life, for death.
Which will arrive first?
Will he ever see this child, their third?

The following day, she doesn't arrive as usual.
Instead there is a telephone call
from his colleague in the maternity unit.
'Congratulations! You have a daughter.'

Nobody knew where he found the strength
to get up from his death-bed.
He surprised them all as he entered the room,
where his wife was nursing the new-born.

He took the baby in his arms,
and for a short while they were together:
the three of them,
united by a sheer, ephemeral joy.

'Will you call her Ann?' he said, handing her back.
'Ann Margareta Maria.'
He knew he would never see his daughter again.
This was the moment he'd been holding on for.

The baptism took place the day after his funeral.
They gave her the names he had requested.

Such was my entry to life,
the heritage I carry.
He was my father.
And I was his last-born child.

I found my neighbour in tears by her cattle-shed.
She looked tired and dishevelled,
her clothes were stained with mud and blood.

'We lost the calf,' she wept in answer to my question.
'A fine bull calf. Everything was perfect.
The little hooves, tail, ears; teeth and all.'

Are calves born with teeth? I asked myself
but I didn't say so.
I sympathised with her sadness,
having once shed a few tears myself
over a Charolais calf
still-born for no better reason
than the vet being out of reach.
I remember the sight
of the strong muscular body in its golden hide.
The uncomprehending look of the mother
as she licked him, expecting life.

My neighbour was convulsed by a sob.
'Such a beautiful creature –
and only fit to be buried.'

I thought of her forebears:
generations of women in rural Ireland,
some of them still living,
who gave birth to still-born children
because they didn't have access
to the medical services they required.
Their babies were taken away
in the dead of night
to be buried by the men
in unconsecrated ground:
secret little graves,
soon overgrown and forgotten.

I imagined the depth of those mothers' grief,
the searing pain of loss;
a nameless tragedy shared by no one.
'Such beautiful creatures –
and only fit to be buried.'

And I wondered,
would those women have wept
over a calf?

The closest I have ever come to the mystery of life:
a Premature Baby Unit.
Watching a tiny scrap of life in intensive care
struggling in agony for each breath.

Twice already he has given up
and had to be resuscitated.
The staff say they can do no more.
The rest is up to him.

Twelve hours ago he was safe from harm.
Comfortable, secure,
in the warm embrace of his mother's womb.
This is what he got instead.
He is alone.
A sign says '*No Touching*'.
Each part of him is either punctured by a needle
or attached to an instrument.
Only his suffering cannot be treated.

'Why would he want to live?' I say to the nurse.
'What attraction could life hold out to him?'
She smiles.
'He's getting the best possible start.
From his point of view,
things can only get better.'

At that moment, the sun rises:
a big orange on the winter horizon.
A ray of hope falls on my newborn son,
and suddenly, his breathing seems less laboured.

By the end of the day, he is out of danger,
sleeping for the first time peacefully.
Dreaming, it appears – of what?
Laughing out loud – why?

In the short time he's been with us,
he's known nothing but pain.
Yet some secret memory is keeping him amused;
giving him the courage
to take on this life,
knowing the suffering
it contains.

So – life is a journey:
a hazardous voyage of discovery;
and we must negotiate our passage
past adversity and trauma
undaunted like a stream rippled by jagged rocks
on its steady descent to the sea.

But it's easy to lose heart;
especially when you are caught
in the bewildering limbo
between the death of the old
and the birth of the new.

That's when we have to remember
Phoenix who rose, time and again,
from the ashes of the past.
Take comfort from the knowledge
that we have bypassed the greatest peril of all:
that of stagnation.

The ancients looked on each crisis as a blessing:
a liberation, the enforced breaking
of new ground.
Favourable to them was anything
that helped our progress
from darkness to light.

There are even those who claim
that extraordinary afflictions
are not the punishment for extraordinary sins
but the trial of extraordinary graces
bestowed on a favoured few.

Looking back, you may well agree
that some of your worst experiences
did in fact carry within them
the seed of something good.

Relish the shadows you leave behind.
They add depth and definition.
For expansion, though, look forward:
into the dazzling new dimension
of the unknown.

You'll see that there are no endings in life.
Only beginnings.

Identity

A place where I had never expected to find myself:
the ancient city of Philippopolis,
capital of Thrace.
A well preserved amphitheatre,
golden in the morning sun.

All alone, I look around:
light and shadow playing on the massive stone structure.
Rows upon rows of concentric stone circles
divided into equal sectors:
some reaching for infinity,
others anchored by the transversal of the stage,
in a balanced blend of growth, reality and potential.

Hovering somewhere near the centre of the circle,
I try to work out why it seems so familiar.
Like being back in my very own landscape.
Though I know that I have never been in Thrace before.
Not in this life – or any other.

No – it's not the location;
it's the configuration.
The geometric concept that produced the amphitheatre:
a Greek marriage of structure and drama
perfectly arranged.

Ever since it first entered my consciousness
- whenever that may have been –
this figure has persisted as my guiding star.
The ideal I always reached for.
Definition of my aims.
It led to architecture, theatre, astrology.
Conditioned every word I wrote.

The essence of my mind in three dimensions
graphically depicted by the amphitheatre.
It took a long time to arrive at that picture.
But it was worth waiting for.

I am a transnational.
One of those people
who leave their country of origin,
sacrifice the security of birth right,
give up an established identity
honed by background and education.

All for the dubious pleasure of starting anew,
unconditioned, unencumbered,
naked as the day you were born;
even at the price of being relegated
to the bottom rung of the social ladder.
Everyone, down to the beggar in the street
- provided he is in his own country -
is better placed than a recently arrived
immigrant.

Initially you struggle along,
ignorant of procedures that all others take for granted,
stuttering in flawed idioms, unable to assert yourself,
unwittingly violating established codes and customs.
You behave, and you are treated,
like someone mentally and socially deficient.
Courtesy and respect are in short supply.

As a clever immigrant you pick up the challenge
and do your best to assimilate,
fast and furiously,
until your new countrymen can no longer tell
that you're not 'one of them'.
But is that really what you want?
Go through life masquerading
as something you are not, and never will be:
'one of them'?

The whole point of migrating,
which by far outweighs the hardship,
is the freedom it brings.
The privilege of not being expected
to conform.
The advantage of belonging
to all cultures and none.
Choosing the best from each one you sample
but at heart remaining
your own unaffected self.

We all love people who represent an image:
who take to life as if it were a stage.
Acting out impressions we can easily interpret,
taking their bow from the rest of us.

Some of them become cult figures:
Evita, James Dean, Kennedy,
Elvis, Grace, Hendrix, Diana –
the list is long.
But there are also modest examples
of people pursuing symbolic lives
in relative obscurity.

I'm sure you can think of a few examples
of people who have successfully invented themselves:
the perfect housewife
ensconced in her colour-matched home,
the businessman in a tailored suit
taking his seat in the board-room.
The bearded bohemian, the stern intellectual,
the sweet-smiling bimbo, and so on.
All helping us decipher the mystery of human nature
by labelling themselves
unequivocally.

In my younger days I worshipped such people,
mistaking for self-realisation
masks cultivated by their owners
to the point where they lost touch
with their own reality.
Perhaps that was the reason why they all died young?

I didn't see the connection.
Mourning my lost idols,
I did my best to follow
in their footsteps.
Until the day when a wise person told me:

'Don't be tempted to live by an image.
It's a much too dangerous game.
To survive in this world you need substance.
And an image is no more substantial
than a dream.'

When did you last hear someone sighing:
'Those were the days.'
Was it a middle-aged woman in clothes too young for her,
humming her favourite golden oldie,
or a weathered man who still wears his hair long
and speaks in the idiom of twenty years ago?
Or – was it your own voice you heard?

You may well be one of many
who are caught in a time warp
maintaining an old-fashioned style;
as if, at some stage, your watch had stopped,
and everything since passed you by.

We all have traces of it,
this urge to halt the passage of time;
whether it is a wish for eternal youth,
a nostalgic hankering for things gone by,
or a vain attempt to defer the final curtain.

But then there are those
who cling to an outgrown persona,
because it is the only one they trust.
They seem to be afraid to mature and develop;
accept that each given moment
offers and adds something new.

What deep insecurity lies behind such fear?
Was there in their past but one occasion,
when they came vibrantly alive?
When they felt, finally,
that they were loved and valued:
someone with a right to be?

Whatever the reason, there is no escaping the fact
that life is all about change and growth.
You are now a somewhat different person
from when you started reading this text.

'No one can bathe in the same river twice.
Because everything flows.'

21

At six years of age,
stunned by grief,
I left my first home,
not expecting to return.

In those days it was considered healthy
to turn your back on pain.
Never look back, but build a bright new future
with whatever was at hand.

I grew up with a void in my heart:
an ever-present sadness that I did not understand.
I thought it had always been there.
Part of my constitution.
Until I went back.

The land between the lakes looked the same,
on one side, Little Lee,
frosty surface glittering in sunlight
within a frame of golden reeds
streaked by long blue shadows from snow-laden trees.
This was our playground in winter and summer –
a haven of childhood serenity.

To the north, guarded by dark forests,
shrouded by purple cloud rising as the ice settled,
the vast deep waters of Large Lee
stretched into the unknown.
Menacing, but at the same time
powerful; majestic.
The steep shores, forbidden ground,
were dangerously attractive.

Spanning these two was the space
where my character formed,
my picture of the world developed.
My cradle -
the cradle we never outgrow,
although we often deny it.

Tears filled my eyes,
as the wound inside me slowly began to heal.
For the first time in forty years
I knew the feeling
of being whole.

Gender

It seems to me there is no such thing
as a sexually liberated woman.
Liberation exists between two people
or not at all.

As a concept it is by all means present
in the heads of innocent young girls,
who proudly look upon their bodies
as assets to be enjoyed.

Unlike her mother, who regarded sex
with shame and fear, through a romantic haze,
today's woman is a free spirit,
confident in her attractions.
She walks at ease into the waiting world
to sample what it has to offer
on equal terms with the men.

Chances are, she may hook a fellow
who can't conceive of such a thing
as women's sexual liberation,
but simply sees a female offering herself for free.

Depending on his level, such a man will either
take advantage, break her heart,
or impregnate, deceive, abandon,
use, abuse, degrade, exploit her;
go as far as beat or rape her.

Years later the woman will look back,
wondering what destroyed her.
Whatever happened to her sexuality?
Her confidence?
Not to mention her attractions?

It has to be said that those lucky few
who team up with a like-minded partner,
go on to have the best of all relations,
whether a fling or a lifetime commitment:
an equal match of balance and respect,
of shared pleasure and mutual enjoyment.

So – all aspiring liberated young women:
Be very careful in your choice of mate,
even for a one-night stand.

In one of our great Victorian novels
I read the following pronouncement:
*"The terrible curse of being poor
is that we cannot afford to protect our women."*

In the old days, rich ladies never moved without an escort,
while the women of the poor were sent into the world
little more than children, vulnerable, exposed,
fair game to anyone.

When I grew up, my mother told me
it was unseemly for young girls
to go about alone at night
or travel without an older companion.

I scoffed at such ridiculous conventions
designed to keep demure young ladies in control.
I was a child of the late twentieth century,
intending to suit myself.
See the world, go where I pleased, at any hour I fancied.

I can recall the thrill of freedom
hitching a lift down the German motorway;
solitary strolls through the Latin Quarter
in the early hours of the morning;
Rome's illuminated baroque churches,
splendid in the dead of night.
Though once in London's Soho I got lost.
A real thug helped me to a taxi,
saying I wasn't safe there on my own.

28

In newspapers we read reports of women
missing, raped or murdered,
having mistakenly believed they were safe.
The truth is, we are still as vulnerable unprotected.
It's not just old-fashioned prejudice
that comes in the way of our freedom.
And not just fear of misbehaviour
that makes our loved ones want to shelter us.

I know now that I was incredibly lucky.
Some women weren't.
To them, and their families,
the danger became real.

Even in our enlightened days,
the saying goes
that women give sex for love.
while men give love for sex.

It makes me think of a modern-day Casanova,
who specialised in entering the homes
of attractive, successful single women as they slept.

Once awake, they were subjected
to a terrifying ordeal
of reassurance, tenderness, affection.
In the end he gently coaxed them into bed:
no sign of force or violence.
Indeed, he did his best to satisfy them;
a few asked him to come back.

Eventually found out, he went on trial
accused of countless serial rapes.
The prosecution had a hard time
getting victims to testify.
They were so deeply ashamed –
not of having been raped,
but of having offered no resistance.

The defence claimed all encounters had been consensual.
His only crime was that of entering people's homes.
The man himself said he just wished
to introduce these lonesome women
to the nature of true love.
The only way to open up their hearts of steel
was by catching them off guard.
One day they'd thank him for easing off
their armour of cold self-sufficiency.

The victim impact reports were decisive.
His actions obviously left them with a trauma
as bad as the most vicious, violent attacks.

He was given a long prison sentence.
And a whole female population
breathed a sigh of relief.

Women said to marry well often marry badly.
I pity any bride who receives congratulations
on having caught an eligible man.
For this implies that she has somehow
got more than she deserves;
that her groom had been expected
to attract something better.

Whether it is looks, age, wealth or education,
background, status or any other mundane criteria,
by which the world measures human value,
the message comes across clearly:
she is lucky; he is not.

It doesn't augur well for the woman's future.
She'll be condemned to a life-long struggle
trying to prove them all wrong:
showing her husband's family and friends
that he didn't make a mistake in choosing her.

The battle is hard to win,
for no amount of hard work,
self-sacrifice or moral rectitude
will ever change the facts of her beginnings;
gain her the esteem initially denied her.

She will always have difficulty asserting herself,
even within her own family.
Children detect such weakness
and are quick to take advantage,
which will further undermine her confidence.

Think of any spoilt, indulged or unruly children you know.
Aren't they usually the product of a mother
unsure of her role in the home?

It's interesting how this trap,
in which so many women are caught,
does not seem to swallow up men.

All one can say is:
No woman should be allowed to marry,
before she knows her own full worth.

On television I saw a program about zebras.
Apparently, within a large herd,
the males look after their families.
Each one has a few females and foals,
for whom he is responsible.

He leads them, drives them and directs them,
shelters and protects them;
seeks out water and new pastures;
takes the front-line in face of any danger.

It struck me that, not so long ago,
such was the role of males in our society.
Men were figures of authority:
instructors, guardians, providers –
at home if nowhere else.

Now with women's independence,
patriarchs are dying out.
Instead we have two partners sharing the load.
Much more satisfactory – for the women.
And, I suppose, some men.

But what about all those males,
shy, insecure, uncertain of their masculinity,
who, unsupported by their culture, fail to make the grade?
Self-assured girls pick their mates with cruel distinction:
usually favouring those strong, able and aggressive.

Think of all the myriad single mothers:
for each one there is a man who in days gone by
would have been the head of her household.
Where are all these obsolete men?
What becomes of them?
Are they gay?
Lonely? Desperate?
Part of suicide statistics?

Somewhere in the course of evolution
a human strand has been lost
and a pool of victims created.

People

I was every bully's dream.
They were drawn to me like bees to honey.
Such easy game:
I must have been irresistible.

The minute someone wilfully attacked me,
verbally or physically,
I broke right down, burst into tears:
submission, humiliation complete.
Bully's mission accomplished.

How I hated myself for being so weak!
For not being able to stand up for myself.
It left me with a deep sense of shame.

I was too young to know that it isn't weakness
to feel aggrieved as you discover
brutality where you expected friendship,
duplicity where you had placed your trust,
malice where you had felt devotion.

As I grew up I learnt that this particular despair
was not really on behalf of my own person.
I felt - still feel - that same lump in my throat
whenever faced with human iniquity:
tales of tortured kittens,
gratuitous violence;
documentaries on the Holocaust;
reports of current war atrocities.

However, my lament is not for the victims,
whose souls no wanton cruelty can touch;
but for those misguided wretches,
who deliberately have taken their leave
of the only thing worth living for:
the only thing that gives life value.

Rejecting and negating human kindness,
they've placed themselves beyond its reach.
For them there is no hope, no redemption.

Now, as my tears fall for them,
I am no longer ashamed.

A friend of mine had been tyrannised
by a formidable mother since the day she was born.
She lived under an emotional terror-reign,
where guilt was the main offensive weapon.
It seemed she couldn't blink an eye
without causing her mother to be
hurt, upset, annoyed, distressed or worse.

'I can't take any more,' she told me in despair.
'My life is spent apologising to my mother.'

'It has to stop,' I agreed.
'You are an adult independent woman.
It's time you told her once and for all
that her emotions are her own responsibility.
No one has a right to blame others
for what they feel.'

She heeded my advice.
The message, apparently, was received
with ice-cold equanimity.

Some time later, my friend gave a recital -
she is a very talented musician.
Her mother, as usual, attended,
and afterwards, with relish,
pulled her daughter's performance to pieces,
adding, for good measure, quotes from the audience:
scathing, humiliating remarks
that she purported to have overheard
in the ladies' room.

Her sweet, gentle daughter burst into tears.
'Mummy, don't say any more,' she pleaded.
'Surely you realise how much it hurts.'

Her mother turned a beady eye on her:
'Don't blame me, dear, for your emotions.
You said it yourself:
they are your responsibility.'

'No,' said my friend, reached by a sudden insight –
perhaps the most important one she'd had.
'That rule does not apply
when someone hurts you intentionally.'

I can recall being eaten with envy.
It made me feel quite ill.
The object was a girl in my school:
blonde, dynamic, with glittering green eyes.
Beyond being beautiful,
she was wonderfully self-possessed.
What else could a teenager wish for?

Her smugness irritated me no end.
She was so radiant, so full of fun,
so damned pleased with life.
Everyone adored her, except me
and a few others equally afflicted.

I nearly fainted the day she came to me
requesting, would I be her friend?
Seemingly sincere, she claimed to be in awe
of my prowess in the classroom,
where she herself had to struggle.

Resentment gave way to devotion.
I became her faithful servant
sunning myself in her glory;
she my loyal supporter boosting my fragile self.
It was a friendship made in heaven,
forged for life.

Sadly, like many flares burning brightly,
hers was not made to last.
Shortly after her nineteenth birthday,
without warning,
she died.

It struck me then as absurd
that, of the two of us,
she should be the one who perished,
while I was the one who was spared.
I had always regarded her as the one who was privileged;
myself as the one deprived.

I thought of my former envy and realised
that, since we don't know what's in store
for any of us,
envy is never justified.

With marital breakdown and single parenthood increasing,
step-families are becoming more and more common.
Such relationships are never easy.
Indeed, the worst mistake people make
is to pretend they are.

Having witnessed the powerful emotions
ruling the responses of those involved
in family arrangements not of their choosing.
I can't help noting, with interest

that women who have a family and re-marry
tend to be apologetic to their new partner
for saddling him with another man's issue;
whereas a man with a family
is much more likely
to be apologetic towards his progeny
for replacing their mother
in his affections.

In the first instance, children are made to feel
that they are an undesired, undesirable appendage;
in the other, the children appoint themselves
critical, resentful judges
of their father's new wife:
an advantageous spot from where to call the shots.
Neither is conducive
to harmonious co-existence,
or a healthy psychological climate.

We all need the family
as a comfortable and secure base camp:
a place to prepare for life's battles
and recover in between campaigns.

All members of a troop
have an equal right to its facilities.
So let's forget about apologizing.
Support each other,
irrespective of blood ties,
the way no one else will.

No matter how placid and peaceful you are,
it will occasionally happen
that people you have no reason to dislike
turn out to be your enemy.
Go out of their way to spite and slander,
sabotage your best efforts;
injure where it hurts most.

Like any decent person,
you will react to such unexplained hostility
by searching deep into your memory
to find the underlying reason.
What could you have done to provoke such antagonism?
Stepped on a tender toe?
Missed an important message?
You'll be eager to put things right.

That won't be easy, however, ,
if the crime of which you're guilty
is, simply, to be yourself:
something you'd be at pains to alter.

There are people who will detest you
for the way you look, or talk, or smile.
Nothing to do with unpleasant characteristics,
wrongdoings or shortcomings.
Usually it is your very best qualities
that are causing the annoyance.

People of the kind who take offence
where no offence is meant
also tend to cultivate hatred
of anyone better adjusted.
They'll never forgive you
and they'll see to it that you're punished.

When you next have a run-in
with one of these,
don't let it upset you.
Just run as fast as you can,
taking care to remind yourself
that you're not the one with a problem.

Feelings

The national conscience
has been shattered by revelations
of the ill-treatment of children
in religious institutions.

Inconceivable but true:
the most vulnerable members of our society,
who, for a variety of reasons,
did not receive their rightful share
of love, care and protection,
were incarcerated in homes,
stripped of identity,
left to starve and suffer,
prey to predators who abused them.

The authorities knew about their plight
but did little to relieve it.
Why should anybody care
about children of no consequence?
They did not even have a vote!

The knowledge is disturbing
but eased by the excuse
that it all happened a long time ago.
Thankfully, things have changed.

Nowadays, the most vulnerable members of our society,
who, for a variety of reasons
do not receive their rightful share
of love, care and protection,
are sent out into the streets,
stripped of identity,
left to starve and suffer,
prey to predators who abuse them.

The authorities know about their plight
but do little to relieve it.
Why should anybody care
about children of no consequence?
They do not even have a vote!

It takes more than a public outcry
to change the way decision-makers feel
about those wretches
whose welfare depends on them.

A Connemara hotelier wrote a furious letter
to the County Manager
complaining that, in his area,
renowned for outstanding natural beauty,
major road repairs were consistently carried out
in the height of the tourist season.
If this wasn't sabotage, he growled,
it was an example of extreme
professional insensitivity.

The County Engineer replied,
politely and regretfully,
explaining that they had no option
but to repair the roads in summer,
as otherwise the tar wouldn't set.

The hotel owner laughed when he told the story.
 'Years of anger and frustration –
and all due to my own ignorance!'

I was reminded of a man I knew,
whose childhood had been overshadowed
by the fact that, aged eight,
he had been dispatched to boarding-school.
Nobody had bothered to tell him
that, in families like his, this was normal practice.
He assumed he must have done something terrible
to forfeit the right to his home
and to his parents' love.

Even after he grew up and got his facts straight,
the feeling of rejection persisted.
So much suffering, completely unnecessary,
again due to ignorance.

It's staggering to think that, at this moment,
countless lives and relationships
are being ruined
by virulent, destructive feelings
generated by misconceptions.

If only everyone ensured
that they were properly informed,
before allowing a feeling to take root,
the world wouldn't be full of fools
barking up the wrong tree!

The doorbell rang.
A friend walked in, pale and shattered.
Dark rings under red-rimmed eyes.
Lips quivering from restrained emotion.
'She's left me,' he whispered,
as if expecting the words to hurt.
'After fourteen years of an ideal marriage,
she's upped and left me.'

I couldn't help thinking of his wife
telling me in confidence
that the marriage, to her, was a prison:
a locked cell, stifling and restrictive;
no access to daylight or fresh air.
'I shall have to break out,' she stated calmly,
'or else go under.'

'I love her,' he said brokenly.
'Since the day we met, I've only lived for her.
My life was dedicated to her welfare.
Without her, I have nothing.'

It crossed my mind that this degree of spousal devotion
seems to come more naturally to men.
I wonder if it stems from an unconscious yearning
back to the blessed state of infancy,
when all their requirements were filled
by a bountiful madonna
who asked for nothing but submission
in return.

'Could it be,' I ventured carefully,
in an attempt to help, if not comfort,
'that your relationship has been based
on your needs more than hers?'

'Not at all,' he snapped, offended.
'I never had a thought for myself.
I gave her everything, each living moment.
Body and soul, I was all hers.'
Bewilderment took over, as he pondered:
'How can any woman walk away
from such devotion?'

I didn't have the heart to tell him.
Perhaps one day I will.

Of all emotions, the most dangerous
are those we don't know we have.
They are the cause of rash, impulsive acts;
they drive us to be erratic,
eliminate our sense of judgement.

It's natural enough to want to close the door
on feelings that are painful or unworthy.
But suppression has an awful lot to answer for
in terms of devastation.

By contrast, there's the other kind:
erupting at short notice,
making us scream and shout,
laugh or cry,
with little or no restraint.

One thing is certain:
the more strongly a feeling manifests itself,
the more superficial it is.
Using moods to let off steam,
indulge ourselves,
or even to manipulate others,
is a means to an end
not altogether honourable.

Emotional responses need not affect our conduct.
Like spoilt children, they crave attention,
but once we recognize them,
they settle down

leaving us free to accept them as being there,
though of no more importance to our life
than the twinge you register
when a needle pricks your finger.

The purest, most sacred feelings
are those we encounter
deep inside ourselves
in moments of peace and solitude.
Such feelings crave no tribute;
they answer to no needs.
They are, in themselves,
what we consist of.

Forgiving an enemy
is but a sweet pleasure.
After all, it is entirely in your own interest
to rise high above your adversary
in integrity and dignity.
Nothing crushes a person of ill will
like the opponent's magnanimity.

It's different when a loved one inflicts a wound,
lets you down,
tramples all over your heart.
How could you forgive them?
That would lessen the impact
of the damage done,
play down the transgression;
almost, you might say, condone it.

What you really want is to compound their guilt,
draw attention to the crime
for which no remorse is sufficient.
Punish them for your pain,
even at the expense of destroying
your own self.

Bitterness is a disease;
the only cure forgiveness.
But not everyone is capable
of summoning the inner strength
required for such a feat.

A safer bet by far
is to forestall situations
that call for forgiveness
by acknowledging hurt
openly and honestly,
at an early stage:
before it begins to fester.

For your own part, make sure
that nothing you say or do
could give rise
to such deep resentment.

It is the need for forgiveness,
as much as the lack of it,
that kills relationships.

Love

During a brief acting career,
I appeared in an obscure play
at a backstreet theatre.
My part was a real challenge,
furiously rehearsed for weeks.

On the second night after opening,
I was aware of a strange lack of response from the house.
Believing there was something lacking in my performance
I tried a little harder – and harder still.
No improvement.

Only in the interval was the terrible truth revealed:
There was no one in the audience.
I was mortified.
To this day I feel the blush on my cheek
when I think of myself pouring my heart out
to no one.

I quit acting soon after that.
It obviously wasn't the right choice for me,
if a tribute was so essential.

Just think of an artist like Renoir,
who went on producing pictures,
day in day out, year after year, decade following decade.
Nothing ever stopped him,
no amount of discouragement, poverty or failure.
He painted away, in pure delight at his own creativity,
regardless of people's opinions.

To be an artist merely for the return it may bring
is as doomed as entering a relationship
only for what you hope to get out of it:
warmth, togetherness, intimacy, sex,
security, money, status or whatever:
The minute the reward is not forthcoming,
it all comes to an end.

Love is like art:
to survive it has to be genuine,
exist on its own merits,
undaunted by scorn or rejection,
and never requiring an applause.

A lot of people have a fear of commitment.
I suppose what they really abhor
is becoming dependent,
handing over control.
I can relate to that.

What I can't understand is why anyone
should want to control another,
especially in the name of love.
If you attempt it,
it leaves the other person with no option
but to resist, evade or deceive you,
or, worst of all, succumb to your will,
in which case their personality expires,
and you are stuck with what?
A mollusc.

The symbiosis of domination,
like any mutual dependence,
is the enemy of love.
Based on want, our greatest weakness,
it makes us stunted, insecure.
For if you rely on each other
to fill the vacuum inside you,
one of you is always bound to lose,
as the other one dies, or simply moves on.

So – if you wish to find a partner:
foster your independence,
overcome your needs.
Thus released, you'll have the best to offer:
your own affluent heart.

Give freely of your love,
until you come across another giver.
Then it will all fit,
without any restrictions.
You'll both be ready for the ultimate gift:
that of commitment.

Trivia is poison for the soul.
It wears you down,
grates on your nerves,
drives you to distraction.

Mental breakdowns and stress-related illness
are often due to pressures
of the most meaningless kind.

As for romance, few antidotes are as effective
as the trials and tribulations
of normal, everyday family life.
Before you know it,
endless concerns of little or no significance
take up your entire field of vision.

It takes something extraordinary,
perhaps a brush with tragedy,
to make you aware of what you stand to lose.

When a friend of ours died unexpectedly,
leaving behind a wife and a young child,
I wrote the following lines to my husband:

My love, when you die –
if you die before me –
I shall grieve.
Not for your passing;
I know better than that.
What can't be altered
must be borne
and gracefully accepted.
But I shall grieve –
oh how I shall grieve
for each moment of our life together
that we had and did not treasure:
precious gifts left unopened,
blossoms trampled underfoot.
Celebrations
lost forever.
Sacrificed.
Waylaid.
Oh my love, how I shall mourn them.

Many years ago in London,
I was visited by a girl-friend
in a highly emotional state.

I was used to seeing her troubled,
plagued by doomed or thwarted expectations,
often lonely and depressed.

It transpired that she'd been to a seance.
A male voice had sought her out,
telling her, tenderly, how much he loved her,
how he wished to see her happy,
and how he was always watching over her.

'It was my father,' she whispered tearfully.
'The father I never knew.
He died when I was a baby.'

What nonsense, I thought to myself.
To her I said:
'Surely there's no such thing as spirits.'

'Be that as it may,' she smiled, unperturbed.
'The thing is, it made me realise
that he must have loved me like that.
And, although he's gone,
I still have his love.
It is contained within me.
I just wasn't aware of it before.'

The girl I knew had been transformed.
She stood before me radiant,
lovable and loved.
As I looked at her, I was in no doubt
that the person she had suddenly become
had a rosy future ahead of her.

That moment was a turning-point
for me, too.
For, just like her, I had a father
who died when I was a baby.

My son used to have a black-and-white pet rabbit
who amazed us all.
He was fully house-trained,
answered to his name;
he played with dinky toys
and went cycling in a basket on the handle-bars.

He liked watching the early evening news,
sitting on the sofa with the rest of us,
occasionally operating the remote control
with his hind paw,
or sipping tea from my mug when I wasn't looking.

The rabbit was so much part of our life,
we couldn't imagine it without him
scuttling around the house.

After two years he was struck down with 'flu.
The nasty kind that few rabbits survive.
I rang the vet, who promised to come:
a sixty mile round-trip for our precious pet.

While waiting, I took the rabbit on my lap
to try and syringe some water into him.

Weak, but peaceful, he lay on his side
in what seemed an unnatural position.
He placed his head comfortably on my arm
and gave me a curious glance:
not like a rabbit at all.

Later I realized it was an acknowledgement:
of my presence, my care, and my love for him.
For at that moment I had a rare sensation
of love in its purest, most unadulterated form:
love stripped of all self-interest,
existing only as a mystic force.

I felt it reaching out from me,
enveloping the tiny body on my lap
like a protective mantle,
holding him as gently as my arms,
while he breathed his last.

I shall never forget the rabbit
or the feeling he, like any living thing,
was able to inspire.

Motherhood

In springtime, when our first lambs arrive,
I look at the ewes,
see them nursing their young,
tenderly, contentedly,
licking the wet coats,
bleating reassuringly.

And I say to myself,
how basic the maternal instinct is.
Being a mother is easy;
all you have to do is follow your nature.
No call for balanced judgements,
knife-edge decisions;
you just do what comes naturally.

Before long, however,
motherhood takes on another aspect:
When your treasure turns her innocent gaze on you and says
'no'.
Spits out the nourishing good food you have prepared for
her,
stamps her little foot
and announces that she hates you.

If you were a sheep,
this is when you'd decide
that time has come for weaning;
turn your back on the offspring
and enjoy chewing your grass in peace,
without someone tugging at your udder.

We, of course, can't do that.
Our children need us, more than ever,
once the maternal bond starts to give.

To love them just as much can be a challenge.
But this is where we start to learn from our young:
lessons of respect and tolerance and understanding.

Being a mother is no longer easy.
But it is more rewarding.

Once I found myself in an air emergency.
Before attempting to crash-land,
we had to spend an hour circling
to burn up excess fuel.

It was a very long hour.
The stranger in the seat next to me held my hand
and told me his whole life
was passing in front of his eyes.

My own mind was following a more morbid course,
picturing my funeral,
pondering whether there would be enough left of me
to put in a coffin.

Then another thought broke through,
the agonising thought
my unconscious had been fighting to suppress:
the toddler I had left behind,
the image of him
coming into our bedroom in the morning,
getting into his mother's bed
to start the day with a cuddle.

I saw him entering this room day after day,
with a bed that remained empty,
where he would never again
feel his mother's arms
wrapped around his warm little body.

It was then that I realised
the terrible encumbrance of parental love.
How it ties us in fetters to this life,
holds us to ransom,
so that we can't even die gracefully,
without our hearts being broken.

Since that day, I have only one prayer for myself:
that I may live long enough
to see my child able to get on without me.

My only child
has just started boarding-school.
The house is painfully empty.
It was the boy himself who wanted to go,
backed up by his father.

I resisted, with rational arguments
and less rational emotions.
In the end I confronted my husband and asked him
why he wanted to send our son away to school.
'Because I believe he would benefit,'
was his straight answer.

In the sleepless night that followed,
I had to admit that he was right.
By daybreak I had accepted that,
whatever my own feelings,
I had no right to hold up a process
that would assist my child
in his social and academic development.

And I remembered the lines
my mother wrote in a notebook
the day I left home
to study in a foreign country:

When you were born,
I said to myself,
I shall never again be alone.
Little did I realise
that the infant I cradled in my arms
was given to me on loan,
to care for and prepare
for the day when I would hand him over,
to another life
that I can share
only from a distance.

'Something only a mother could love.'
The phrase conjures up images
of baby orang-utans, teenage hoodlums;
vicious or repulsive monsters.

It does suggest a mother's love is blind,
oblivious to character disorders,
to ugliness and failings;
when in reality it is the other way round:
maternal love is extraordinarily perceptive.

When a mother looks upon her children,
she sees not only what they are,
but also what they may become.
In her eyes, potential
goes beyond deficiencies.

She is aware of the best in each one
even when it's not apparent.
Her interpretations are kind,
allowing for lapses,
always giving the benefit of the doubt.
It says a lot about human character that,
more often than not,
she's proved right.

Provided she is no stranger
to warm and selfless feelings,
a mother will love her children
for all that is contained within them,
or even, at times, in spite of it;
remaining constant
even in the worst scenarios.

When a child has contrived to destroy
anything in it worthy of affection,
its mother, with deep regret,
will continue to love it,
partly for what it was,
partly for what it might have been.

My mother, aged seventy,
was in a horrific motor accident.
For days she was on life support;
both her legs had to be amputated.

'The poor woman,' said my well-meaning neighbour.
'Wouldn't it be better if she was just left to die?'

Before her last operation,
she was able to talk to me.
'I don't know what I'm fighting for,' she said.
'What sort of life do I have to look forward to,
even if I do survive?'

'That's for you to decide,' I answered.
'Only you can tell whether life in a wheel-chair
would still be worth living.'

She thought for a while about this,
and then she stated:

'What I value most
is having my children.
Follow you as you grow older;
see how your lives develop.
Be there for you when you need me.'

She survived. She recovered.
Today, nine years later, she lives alone,
in an adapted flat,
where her daily routine is much the same as usual,
except, amazingly, she's happier than before:
enjoying a late blossoming.

With a brand new interest to sustain her,
she depends on no one;
her life is her own.

But now and then she remembers
that critical moment,
when a mother's love for her children
made all the difference.

Life

Do you have a main objective?
An overriding ambition that you intend
to get around to one day?
Once the children are grown up,
the mortgage paid, the garden planted?
When you get a better job, retire,
win the Lotto?

We potter away,
consumed by all those little tasks
that keep us from attending
to things that really matter.
Waiting, waiting for the day
when we will finally come into our own.

Frustrated, unfulfilled, we trundle on,
completing one lap after another
on our everyday obstacle course,
while our dreams evaporate on the horizon
and the goalposts keep shifting.

Then, suddenly, an exit appears!
A wide-open path to self-realisation.
Likely as not, we turn the other way:
focus on yet another obstacle.

Is the effort too much?
The shocking impact of sudden change?
Or is it a pathetic fear of failure
that makes us cling to limitations
whenever freedom is within reach?

Fulfilment needn't be a trauma.
You just set your sights within your capabilities,
and then make it a matter of priority,
allowing nothing in the way of your endeavour.

With your eyes fixed upon the target,
you can add a tiny brick each day.
Work away, unnoticed, unperturbed,
until, sooner or later, you see it emerge:

That impressive structure.
Your lifetime achievement.

A man I know is a troubled soul.
Mid-life, he had a breakdown.
In therapy he was told to make a list
of things he felt he couldn't cope with,
and overleaf, write down what he most enjoyed.

'Well done,' said the therapist, as he handed in his list.
'That's the bulk of your work done.
All that remains is for you to decide
what you want to do about all these.'

He started by saying good-bye
to the things he didn't favour:
wife, children, elderly father, drooling dog.
The family home he sold at a handsome profit,
which allowed him to pay off
both wife and hefty mortgage.

His job was next in line:
early retirement on the grounds of ill health.
Then he went to live in a small apartment in Torremolinos,
where he could indulge, all year round,
in the two items on his list of preference:
golf and windsurfing.

If he wasn't entirely happy, he was at least,
at last, in therapeutic parlance,
true to himself.

Two years later he was back in London
receiving treatment for depression.

'This therapist is no good at all,' he complained to me.
'She says my problem is, I'm too selfish.
If I did something to benefit other people,
my health would improve dramatically.
That's a complete contradiction
of what I was taught before!'

'How can I do both?' he exclaimed despairingly.
'Benefit others whilst remaining true to myself?
It's impossible!'
As I said, he is a troubled soul.

'Is there such a thing as fate?'
asked a young man at a party.
A welcome change
from the usual inconsequential chit-chat.

I told him I did not think so –
but I did believe in destiny.
He looked at me perplexed.
'That's the same thing!'

I took a deep breath, but before I could begin,
he had been spirited away by a siren
with long blonde hair and purple finger-nails.
So I never got a chance to tell him

that fate, in my view, is pre-determined,
whereas destiny we hold in our hands.
It's a deliberate fulfilment:
potential moulded by our own free will;
the management of personal resources,
determined by the moves we make
at each juncture, each given moment.

Events may hit entirely unforeseen,
impossible to check, prevent or further.
But the response is up to you.
You decide how it is going to affect you:
externally, internally,
for better, for worse.

See your changing circumstances
as markers on your way.
Maintain a dialogue with them,
and you'll find that you remain in charge.

All this I wanted to say
to the nice young man at the party.
Now he'll have to find his own answers,
which is perhaps as well.

At least he's made a good start
asking that vital question.

As a young adult, having just received
a rewarding but not very marketable arts degree,
I found myself staring vacantly into the abyss of my future.
So many possibilities, so many perils!
Endless potential, for success as well as failure.
Irrevocable choices waiting to be made.
I was caught between fear and desire:
a paralysing dilemma.

Then I was given this advice
by an old family friend,
who himself had excelled in life:

'Base no major decisions
on your own needs and ambitions:
that's like looking at the world
through the wrong end of a telescope.
To succeed you must forget what you want;
instead, develop and offer what you've been given.'

So this was it,
the rite of passage into the great big world:
to look beyond your own person,
accept yourself as a component
consigned to playing your part
in a large universal structure.

I discovered that he was right.
By contributing what I had,
to the best of my ability,
I found the strength and confidence I needed
to go forward.
And if I didn't achieve all that I had hoped for,
the effort brought as much satisfaction
as the result.

Away from personal gratification,
choices are easy.
There are no anxieties, no frustration,
no regrets.
Just the inner peace of knowing
that, whatever happens,
you did your best.

You ask me why I do it.
Why work so hard?
All this pain and exertion
for such fickle returns?

How can I explain to you
that I don't have a choice in the matter?
My work is my conscience,
a whip and a spur.
It drives me out of bed in the morning,
sends me on errands in dark places,
where no one can follow.

What am I searching for?
The spring of *aqua vitae?*
Fuel to feed my fire?
Anything to keep me going.
Keep me alive.

Whenever I run out of steam,
I think of my friends out there:
anyone who would, could, might one day
read and relish what I write.
Unknown thousands -- or just one,
they are my reason,
and my excuse
to continue.

It gets lonely at times
here in this capsule of self-imposed labour,
the nature of which no one seems to understand,
not even those who know me well.
It would take someone like you
who are close enough to see it
from my end.

Don't look upon my work as a rival
taking me away from you,
but a worthy objective,
which, if shared,
will only bring us closer together.

Religion

On principle, I hold with the view
that everyone has a religion.
If you define the word as an inner conviction,
it will include even the atheist, and the agnostic.

Psychology suggests that our relationship with God
is conditioned by our links with authority in general.
Perhaps the truest manifestation of a culture
can be detected in its religious attitudes.

Having said that, I recall being in a shop in Sweden,
ordering something, quoting my home address.
'Ireland?' said the shop-assistant, a spry lady in her sixties.
'What is it like? Any different from here?'

Choosing from a myriad examples,
I told her briefly
that Irish families tend to be larger.
Children could number ten or eleven,
even fifteen, sixteen.

'Sixteen children!' cried the grey-haired lady,
a look of horror on her face.
Then she leant confidentially over the counter
and uttered in a hushed voice:
'Is this because Irish men are particularly...
insistent?'

Smiling, I explained that the Catholic Church
does not approve of family planning:
'It is considered wrong to take such precautions
if it is God's will that a child be conceived.'

'God's will!' she exclaimed. 'But he doesn't exist!'
And then, seeing my baffled face, she went on:
'I mean, that's common knowledge – *nowadays*.

I left the shop, reflecting that here was one person
who was truly void of religion.

My first religious crisis came at the age of seven.
Up until then my relationship with God
had been problem-free.
I liked the idea of a kind father in Heaven
looking after our dear departed,
guiding my step, prompting me to be good,
sending his guardian angel to protect me
against anything nasty or dangerous.

But then I received religious instruction at school.
The teacher was a puritan:
you could tell from her forbidding black dress
and the way her thin grey hair was pulled back
in a tight bun.
The only thing alive on her
was a pair of nut-brown eyes
burning with religious fervour,
and never more so than in divulging the story
of Man's Shameful Fall.

'God knew how to deal with disobedience,'
she announced triumphantly.
'He said to Adam, you'll pay dearly for this.
You will carry the burden of your guilt for ever;
no generation will be spared.
Get thee out of Paradise,
to earn thy bread in the sweat of thy face,
till the day when it pleases me
to turn you to dust!'

Poor Eve fared no better.
She was told she would bear her children
in sorrow and anguish;
her desire would be her wretched husband's:
he would rule over her.

I listened in dismay,
as this new face of God emerged:
mean and vindictive, petty and cruel.
Light-years away from the merciful father
I had got to know and love.

You can't trust anyone,
I concluded despondently.
To fly off the handle like that –
and all for the sake of an apple!

101

There are those who turn to our Lord
only in times of need;
look upon Him as a kind of insurance policy
activated by their humility.

They never doubt their supplications will be heeded,
and they are right - as long as they accept
that no is also an answer;
that delay does not constitute denial;
and that the granting of a request
frequently carries a price tag.

It's not unusual
for people to get exactly what they prayed for
and then spend the rest of their days
wishing they hadn't.

Like friends of mine who were in dire financial straits,
having overextended themselves
building the house of their dreams.
With all avenues of credit exhausted,
they found themselves with three days to produce
ten thousand pounds - or else lose their home.

In desperation, for the first time in decades,
the wife went down on her knees
and pleaded with the God she hardly knew
to send them the required amount.

The next day her husband came home from work
and - miraculously - handed her a cheque
for ten thousand pounds.
It was a redundancy payment.
His job, their sole source of income,
had been lost.

Lacking the perspective
that only hindsight will provide,
we are not ever in a position
to determine what's in our own best interest.
Therefore, we might as well leave it to Providence
to mete out what we deserve,
whilst we pray for the strength of mind
to recognize and honour
our rewards.

When asked about their spirituality,
the first thing Irish people tell you
is how often they go to Mass.

This is not a definitive answer,
but a deep-seated misconception
fostered and encouraged by the church:
'If you're spiritual, you are religious.
If you're religious, you go to church.'

But people go to Mass
for a variety of reasons:
social, cultural, habitual, or merely
out of respect or fear of authority.
The church is just a building,
and an institution
created and ruled by man.

Religion, on the other hand,
is deeply personal:
an individual's relationship with God,
defined by faith and conscience.
It can by all means be expressed through worship,
but thrives as well, if not better,
through word and deed.

Spirituality, again, is something different.
It is reflected in your attitude to life:
what you find in it of value;
how you choose to commune with the world.

Only when each one of these strands
has been separately and honestly unravelled,
can you determine how and if they coincide.
If you are lucky, you will find
that they can all be fused together
through the one medium:
ideally, the church.

As a regular, sincere churchgoer,
you are no more religious or spiritual
than some of those who stay away.
But you will be less lonely.

The cathedral of Saint-Sernin, Toulouse:
a Romanesque masterpiece
built by a faith that moved mountains,
literally, stone by stone;
turning them to arches soaring heavenward,
higher and higher, like souls yearning for release,
in unabashed defiance of existing building techniques.

Seen piecemeal, arch upon arch,
what you perceive is substance;
diverse elements ranged sequentially.
Yet the dynamics wrought
by light and obscurity,
space and matter,
optical illusions,
transform the structure into a single chord:
a keynote deep and sonorous.

Like so many of our disjointed life experiences:
bereft of meaning until you step away
and allow the full picture to emerge.
The picture that, once seen,
is never doubted.

Who said there is no life in stones?
This goes beyond bricks and mortar.
The twelve identical stone vaults
in their ever-diminishing perspective
draw you gently but irrevocably
towards the site of the high altar
reposing within an ambulatory
brimming with brilliant light.

Grace within reach.
Comfort beckoning.
A vision of ultimate peace.
Nine hundred years old
and just as real today.

Faith is fed by many sources.
For me Saint-Sernin is one.

Mind

Have you ever found that, in sharing a memory,
especially with someone you know well,
your recollections differ?
Even within a closed circle,
the records of the past
emerge with astounding discrepancy.

Like the occasion of Mary's wedding:
'What a terrible, stormy day.'
'Not at all – the sun was shining!'
'It was calm, but the rain poured down.'

'And when Billy came back from England
 in his beautiful brand new car...'
'What do you mean, it was an old banger!'
'I'm quite sure he came on the bus.'

One person recalls minute details,
where other minds are blank.
There are as many versions of a story
as there are people telling it.

Perhaps our impressions of things past
tell more about ourselves
than about the actual events?

We all have our own method
of selecting, sorting and storing
files for our personal archives.
The material is uniquely ours:
we are what we remember.

110

But if memories are just individual distortions of the facts,
does it not follow that somewhere, in amongst them,
hides the real truth?
And if we're brave enough to go beyond them,
follow the trail they lay,
it will lead us to the source and, finally, reveal all:

not just what actually happened
but also
how it affected us.

Hillwalking in Connemara,
my guide stopped and pointed
across a broad expanse of barren bogland.

Down there was a townland
with a substantial two-storey house
surrounded by mature trees,
smooth green fields, solid stone walls:
all testimony to erstwhile prosperity.

Apparently, this had not always prevailed.
At one time, a man had lived there on his own,
starving in a hovel, struggling to survive.
Then one night he had a dream that,
if he went to the bridge in Limerick,
his fortune would be made.

With little to lose he set out,
walking for days, until he found the bridge.
He lingered there, but nothing happened.
After three days, a man stopped and asked,
what keeps you here, stranger?

Hearing about the dream,
the Limerick man laughed out loud.
'What would the world be like,
if we all followed our dreams?
I dreamt one night I was in a place called Úraid.
I dug in a place between twin thorn trees
and unearthed a pot of gold.
But never would I be such a fool as to
take any notice of that!'

'Thank you,' said the man from Úraid
and returned home,
to dig in the spot
between the twin thorn trees.
The pot of gold was there;
his fortune was made.

No wonder I'm at home in Connemara:
the land where dreams take precedence.

Do you ever have the strange experience
of remembering things
that haven't yet happened?

Every now and then, impressions come to me,
seemingly insignificant, like a dream recalled:
some parts well-defined, others nebulous.
A distinct atmosphere instantly recognisable
when the event occurs.

The window of an antique shop,
a light rain falling,
myself in a black mackintosh:
The moment came about one day
in Pimlico Road, London.

A magnificent pink camellia
in a sun-dappled conservatory:
I waited half a lifetime
to see that realised.

And for years I was haunted by an unidentified sound
emanating from our hall,
associated with a vague form,
half-endearing, half-annoying,
existing somewhere level with my knees.

The mystery was solved eventually
by my three-year-old pedalling his trike
with an array of noisy toys
attached to the back of it.
Round and round on the flagstones of the hall,
relishing the clatter it created.

These visions make me wonder
if time exists at all.
Perhaps it's just a concept invented by ourselves
to bring order into chaos;
to enable us to learn
lessons from the past?

Or, else, time does exist,
but it stands still,
while we are the ones who keep moving.

In that case, what's the reason
for occasionally moving too fast?

All my adult life I've had the same
recurring dream:

I am standing outside one of the houses
where I used to live in the past,
when I see a road, or a pathway,
leading off to somewhere behind it.

Intrigued, I follow the path,
walk along an avenue of flowering shrubs,
into a village with cobbled streets,
quaint architecture,
cosy inns, pretty little shops:
all very appealing.

Delighted to have found this perfect idyll,
I am also filled with wonder
that I have lived for so long in this place
without ever realizing
what lay behind it.

The feeling of elation persists when I wake up.
It stays with me for days,
fading away only gradually.

In recent times, I have deduced
that this must be my sub-conscious mind pointing out
that fulfilment would have been attainable,
right there on my doorstep,
if I had only taken the trouble
to look for it.

For that is one important thing that I have learnt:
If you don't expect to find it,
you never notice the path to happiness,
even if it's staring you in the face.
My dream makes up for past neglect,
instilling in my memory the joy that was lacking.
The simple joys of life that are always there,
waiting to be discovered.

I suppose it is a good sign
that, with each year,
my dream becomes less frequent.
Even so, I miss it.

'Humble? Me? You must be mad!'
exclaimed my friend,
unwittingly confirming the allegation.
He was a man of grandiose gestures,
a host of sumptuous parties
featured in gossip columns.
But then why should humility be the exclusive domain
of the dull and mousy?

At heart he was quite shy,
the way all sincere people
become self-conscious under scrutiny,
because they have nothing
to cover themselves with:
no affectations, no false veneer.

He confided to me he was in serious financial trouble.
Myself young and poor, I dismissed it:
'Never mind. As long as you have your health.'
He smiled. 'I'd rather be a rich invalid
than a healthy pauper.'
'You'll be all right,' I told him.
'Anyone with your talent for friendship
has little to worry about.'
He was a wonderful friend
to many, many people.

A shadow passed over his face.
'What's the point of having friends
if you have nothing to offer them?'
That's when I accused him, with a laugh,
of selling himself short.
I was too inexperienced to know
that excessive humility
is a serious distress signal.

Anyone who imagines
that his own person stripped of assets
is of no value to others,
also believes that his actions lack the power
to hurt anyone.
It is a most dangerous mindset
and it should never be passed over.

My friend died of an overdose
three days after going bankrupt.

Soul

In my teens I befriended
a neighbour's son called Benny.

Benny was like any normal twelve-year-old.
The only problem was,
his body was over thirty.
But he was happy and good-natured;
I enjoyed his company.

His mother said, he had done well at school.
They all had high hopes for him.
I waited to hear more, and eventually,
with infinite sadness,
she told me about the accident.

Apparently, Benny had had an older brother
whom he idolised.
A kind, protective young man who rode a motor-bike.
One day, entreated by his little brother,
he took him for a spin.

That was the evening when some mindless vandals
had decided to torture a horse,
wrapping its head in loops of barbed wire.
The wretched animal, driven to insanity,
bolted on to the main road,
right in the path of the motor-bike.
Brother and horse were killed on impact.
Benny escaped unhurt.
But he was never the same again.

His mother wiped away a tear.
'It is as if some part of him,
the most vital part,
cannot bear to go beyond that moment.'

I wish we could all do the same:
preserve our innocence,
remain in that sacred space we inhabited
up until the moment of our first confrontation
with evil.

How do you help a person
heading off down the wrong avenue?
The following I wrote to someone close,
whose selfish, destructive manner,
and obsession with her own physical comfort,
had left me deeply concerned.

My dear – where is your soul?
I know it exists,
I remember it from days gone by.
My dear – hold on to your soul!
You can't afford to lose it.

It's easy enough to live by your body's dictates,
succumb to its wishes, follow its every whim.
But sooner or later, the flesh lets your down.
And where will that leave you?

Don't fall for the cruel belief
that the body is all you've got,
but see it as the humble servant of your self:
an obedient tool helping you realise
your highest ambitions.

Forget your matter and seek your soul,
find it, nurture it,
with all means at your disposal.
It is your only protection
against the body's relentless decay
that sets in the moment you're born.

124

You who are no longer young,
be aware that your soul will lift you
above disease and suffering,
pain and degradation,
safeguarding your dignity
until the day you die.

I'm saying this as someone who was there,
who reached the end,
touched her soul,
and glimpsed eternity.

By way of reply she suggested
that I seek professional treatment.

When I look back upon a rich and varied life,
there is one thing I truly regret.
One thing only that I wish could be undone:
trying illegal drugs.

In my day, cannabis was hailed
as the wonderdrug favoured by cool role-models
like the Beatles and Rolling Stones.
A gift of nature, mind-expanding,
unlike the alcohol stupefying our parents
at posh dinner-parties
or violent drunkards beating their wives.
We believed we were the ones who'd got it right.

I don't recall much else from that period,
the flower-power summer of 1967.
I'm hazily aware of some short-lived friendships,
a subtle change of personality,
and an increasingly idle existence.

I soon gave up experimenting,
put off, I imagine, by the rapid intake
of so-called friends into mental institutions
after overtripping on LSD;
and the arrest of some of them
for possession and supply.

Months of inner chaos followed,
turmoil, disarray.
How much of this was due to herbal magic
I shall never know.
And that is what I most deplore.

With all its ups and downs,
life holds one comfort:
it's all exclusively our own,
absorbed into our being,
imprinting its unique design.

But this part wasn't me.
Artificially induced,
it forms a black hole in my consciousness.
A big chunk stolen
from my total life experience.

The earliest myths of many cultures
are based on the theme of dispossession:
the hero who, deprived of his heritage,
fights endless battles
to regain what is rightfully his.

So deeply ingrained is this preoccupation
that, after thousands of years of human development,
it remains a prime concern.

Of course, if we try, we can all imagine
ourselves as dispossessed.
In some respect, at some level,
everyone can conceive a grievance
over entitlements not provided.

It seems a significant portion of humanity
go through life as self-appointed creditors,
convinced that they have somehow been cheated
out of their fair share.
Envy, parsimony, greed -
even theft or addiction –
what are they if not attempts
to redress the balance
between the hand you've been dealt
and the cards you consider owing?

The illusion of dispossession
is often cultivated as a poor excuse
for selfish and unscrupulous behaviour.
Although few things could be less conducive
to personal happiness.

It helps to be aware
that we possess nothing by right.
All we have
- life itself –
is ours by grace alone.

And how many times in the history of mankind
will someone have received
all he believed was his due?

Philosophers agree that human consciousness
goes through different evolutionary stages:

We start as infants at the bottom of the pyramid,
living by instinct and desire.
No awareness of good or evil,
right or wrong.

A lot of people never make it beyond this level.
They go through life like self-motivated robots,
eating, drinking, working, reproducing,
without ever asking themselves why.
Some make a right mess of their conditions:
with nothing but primitive urges to guide you,
it's easy to lose control.

At school-age we learn about discipline,
about adjusting to a social system.
We follow rules, adopt dogma, frequently from our peers,
to the point of fundamentalism.
It's nice and secure to be told what to think,
to be free of personal responsibility.
That's why so many go on to swear blind allegiance
to religion, politics or ideology;
to institutions or all-powerful employers,
to convention and bigotry.

However, those who grow up
to be individuals in their own right
soon start to question other people's values.
At the third level of education,
sceptics and cynics abound.
They do useful work as demolition contractors,
but are less efficient at building things up.

Adulthood comes when we stop reacting
and accept the world on its own terms.
Acknowledge what's beyond the matter:
the miracle of each existence;
the deep significance of being alive.

Only when we arrive at this level of consciousness,
say the philosophers,
does life finally acquire
some meaning.

Death

In failing health, my mother-in-law declared
that she would select for herself
a suitable resting-place.

So one fine Sunday we set out in her car
for a tour of Connemara graveyards.

The one she chose was tucked away on the strand
beneath an ancient church ruin
overlooking a turquoise lagoon.

In return for a bottle of whiskey
and a homemade fruitcake
specially brought for the purpose,
the caretaker promised to reserve the best plot:
'the one with the fairest view'.

Having marked it out with breeze blocks,
we picnicked by her future grave,
enjoying the peace and the beauty
of this wild, remote spot.

'I don't mind at all,' she said, sipping her coffee,
'ending my days on earth,
if it's in a place like this.
Except for the fact that I shall be all alone.'

She was delighted when I vowed
that I'd be buried next to her,
and that she wouldn't have to wait long.
After all, what was thirty or forty years
in the face of eternity?

Only a few months later,
on a stormy October day,
I was back to see her coffin
lowered into the ground.
I thought of our picnic,
and the warmth of that moment
took much of my sadness away.

We go and see her now and then.
And while children and dogs play on the strand,
I draw a peculiar comfort from the fact
that I am visiting my own grave.

I know of someone who was diagnosed
with a terminal illness.
A man in his prime
with a young family.

'This isn't possible,' was his reaction.
'I can't die now.
 I have too much undone.'

And he sat down and made a list
of all the things he wanted to accomplish
before departing from this life.

The doctors were amazed to see
the improvement in his health,
as he worked his way through the items,
ticking them off one by one.

'The question isn't whether or not you live,'
he told me, smiling, on one occasion.
'What matters is how, and why.'

In due course the inevitable happened:
he reached the end of his list.
The illness returned.
Within weeks he had left us,
passed away peacefully.

His story makes me wonder:
is this how it is for everybody?
Do we all have our set agenda,
and when we get to the end of it,
our life is over?

This man was privileged.
He made up his own list.
Most of us have it written for us,
with little say in the matter.

We don't even get to read it,
and only a chosen few
know when we've reached the end.

A member of my extended family
was killed in an accident, aged twenty.

How can you come to terms with that?
How can his parents be expected
ever to come to terms with it?
All those years of caring and nurturing,
seeing him grow and learn –
what were they for?

The only comfort I could find was the thought
that perhaps he wasn't meant to live longer.
His life span, we now know, measured twenty years.
We shouldn't look upon it against the possibility
that it might have been much longer,
but accept the gift of those years
and value them accordingly.

'How do I know that I will survive?'
asked my young son
after learning about his cousin's death.
'You probably will,' I reassured him.
'These days in Ireland, most children do survive.
But no one can be completely certain,
and that is how it has to be.
Because if we could take for granted
that everyone lives to a ripe old age,
we wouldn't treasure each day and each other
quite as much as we do.'

As I said it, my heart went out
to those parents who have to pay the price
for that precious uncertainty.

Let us never forget their pain,
the cross they carry
on behalf of those more fortunate.

On a visit to my native Sweden,
I read a death notice in the paper:
An old friend of mine
had lost her mother.

'The funeral has taken place,' it said.
I learnt later that this wasn't true.
It was put in to discourage mourners turning up.
Some bereaved people like to be left alone
to do their grieving in private.

Even so, I was disappointed.
I would have liked to pay my last respects
to this kindly woman
who had often welcomed me into her home.

My friend gave a cool response,
when I offered my condolences.
She seemed, if anything, embarrassed.
As if death and grief were something shameful.
The ultimate social failure.

I thought of funerals at home in Connemara:
long motorcades escorting the hearse,
wakes lasting through the night,
endless tokens of comfort and sympathy.

And I imagined the lonely figure of my Swedish friend
hunched in a pew in a near-empty church,
harbouring the grief that she wouldn't, or couldn't,
allow anyone to share.

How lucky we are in rural Ireland,
where death is still regarded
as an integral part of life.
The one thing we all have in common
and endure together
in the sombre knowledge
that no one is spared.

When I was nineteen,
I was seriously injured in a car crash.
In fact, I very nearly died.

I remember that night following surgery.
Like many patients in a critical condition,
I found myself passing through a long tunnel:
like being born all over again.
As at birth, a light beckoned at the end,
infinitely alluring.

I would have reached it,
had it not been for the intervention of three nurses.
Three young women whom I'd never seen before
and would never see again.
I recall to this day their eager, youthful faces,
the tears in their eyes as they pleaded with me
to remain in this world a little while longer.

Sartre used to say: hell is other people.
I disagree.
Life is other people.
Those nameless young nurses were speaking,
not for themselves but for others:
Their plea was on behalf of the husband,
the child I would one day have,
and of any other person
to whom my continued existence
would possibly one day make a difference.

It was for them I came back,
for all they had to offer me,
for all I had to offer them:
a decision I've never regretted.

There are times when I long to return
to the stillness and peace of that dark tunnel,
the light shining at the end.
But I know it will still be there for me
when the day comes.

I'm in no hurry.